Made in United States
North Haven, CT
08 June 2023

37488965R00063